S

Festivals *of the* World

CZECH REPUBLIC

Gareth Stevens Publishing
MILWAUKEE

Written by
TIM NOLLEN

Edited by
LEK HUI HUI

Designed by
LOO CHUAN MING

Picture research by
SUSAN JANE MANUEL

First published in North America in 1999 by
Gareth Stevens Publishing
1555 North RiverCenter Drive, Suite 201
Milwaukee, Wisconsin 53212 USA

For a free color catalog describing Gareth
Stevens' list of high-quality books and multimedia
programs, call
1-800-542-2595 (USA)
or 1-800-461-9120 (Canada).
Gareth Stevens Publishing's Fax: (414) 225-0377.

© TIMES EDITIONS PTE LTD 1999
Originated and designed by
Times Books International
an imprint of Times Editions Pte Ltd
Times Centre, 1 New Industrial Road
Singapore 536196
Printed in Malaysia

Library of Congress Cataloging-in-Publication Data:
Nollen, Tim.
Czech Republic / by Tim Nollen.
p. cm.—(Festivals of the world)
Includes bibliographical references and index.
Summary: Describes how the culture of the Czech
Republic is reflected in its many festivals, including
the Prague Spring International Music Festival,
the Chrudim Puppet Festival, and the Burning
of the Witches.
ISBN 0-8368-2031-2 (lib. bdg.)
1. Festivals—Czech Republic—Juvenile literature.
2. Czech Republic—Social life and customs—
Juvenile literature. [1. Festivals—Czech Republic.
2. Holidays—Czech Republic. 3. Czech
Republic—Social life and customs.]
I. Title. II. Series.
GT4871.C9N65   1999
394.2694371—dc21   99-11585

1 2 3 4 5 6 7 8 9 03 02 01 00 99

CONTENTS

It's Festival Time . . .

Are you ready to have fun? Join in some Czech festivals that go back hundreds of years. In the Czech language, the word for festival is *slavnost* (SLAV-nost). Ride horseback with the "kings" or watch puppets spring to life. Then wait for witches to fly on a dark night. Listen to the glorious music of a symphony orchestra in one of the world's most beautiful cities and take part in unique Easter and Christmas celebrations. It's festival time in the Czech Republic!

3

WHERE'S THE CZECH REPUBLIC?

The Czech Republic is a small country in the heart of Europe. In existence only since 1993, it is one of the youngest countries in the world. Before then, it was part of Czechoslovakia, along with the Slovak Republic, which is now the country of Slovakia.

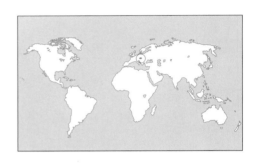

The Czech Republic consists of Bohemia in the west, Moravia in the east, and Silesia in the northeast. Mountains occupy much of the country, so people sometimes call the Czech Republic "the roof of Europe," because many of Europe's rivers start flowing from the mountains there.

These children are wearing traditional Czech costumes.

Who are the Czechs?

Although the Czech Republic is very young, its culture is as old as any other country in Europe. Czech kings ruled Europe in the **Middle Ages**, when Prague, the capital, was called "the Golden City." From 1621 to 1918, the Czech lands were part of the Austro-Hungarian Empire ruled by the Germans. During this time, the people spoke German. Today, however, Germans are a minority in the Czech Republic. Most of the population is made up of Czechs who speak the Czech language. The largest minority group, the Romanies, are commonly called gypsies.

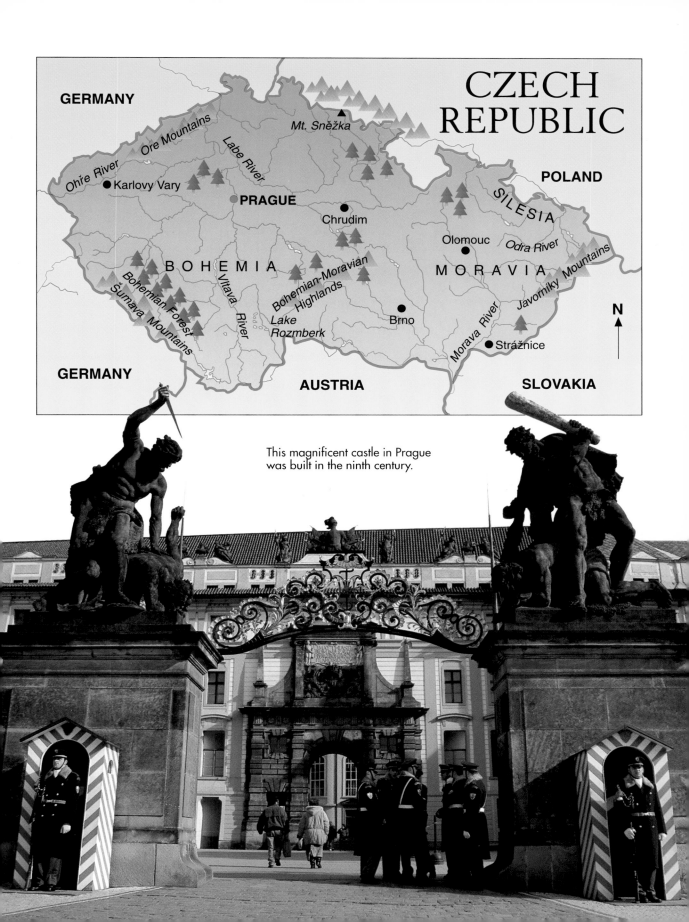

CZECH REPUBLIC

GERMANY

POLAND

GERMANY

AUSTRIA

SLOVAKIA

Mt. Snĕžka

Ore Mountains

Ohře River

Labe River

Karlovy Vary

PRAGUE

Chrudim

SILESIA

Olomouc

Odra River

B O H E M I A

M O R A V I A

Vltava River

Bohemian Forest

Šumava Mountains

Bohemian-Moravian Highlands

Lake Rozmberk

Brno

Javorníky Mountains

Morava River

Strážnice

N

This magnificent castle in Prague
was built in the ninth century.

WHEN'S THE SLAVNOST?

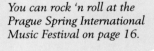

You can rock 'n roll at the Prague Spring International Music Festival on page 16.

WINTER

- ✪ **ST. NICHOLAS' DAY**
- ✪ **CHRISTMAS**
- ✪ **ZABIJAČKA (PIG SLAUGHTER)**—In January, families gather to slaughter a pig. They spend the entire day cooking and eating the pig and singing songs.

SPRING

- ✪ **EASTER**
- ✪ **BURNING OF THE WITCHES**
- ✪ **MAY DAY**—The beginning of spring is celebrated on May 1st. It is also a day when lovers pledge their love to each other.

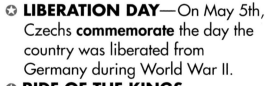

- ✪ **LIBERATION DAY**—On May 5th, Czechs **commemorate** the day the country was liberated from Germany during World War II.
- ✪ **RIDE OF THE KINGS**
- ✪ **PRAGUE SPRING INTERNATIONAL MUSIC FESTIVAL**
- ✪ **OLOMOUC FLOWER FESTIVAL**—The main square of this small city becomes a giant flower garden during this festival.

SUMMER

- ✪ **STS. CYRIL AND METHODIUS DAY**—Czechs celebrate the introduction of Christianity to the Czech lands in the ninth century.
- ✪ **JAN HUS DAY**—On this day, Czechs honor the death of Protestant leader Jan Hus.
- ✪ **ZAHRADA**—This outdoor festival is a celebration of folk and country music.
- ✪ **INTERNATIONAL FILM FESTIVAL**—On the last weekend in June, many famous movie stars arrive in Karlovy Vary for this eight-day film celebration.

- ✪ **CHRUDIM PUPPET FESTIVAL**
- ✪ **CHOD FOLK FESTIVAL**—The Chods are known for their love of walking in the countryside. (Their name comes from the Slavic word meaning "to walk about.") In August each year, the Chods celebrate their culture with a festival of traditional folk dress, bagpipe music, and dance.

AUTUMN

- ✪ **BURČÁK (WINE) FESTIVALS**—These fall harvest festivals celebrate the year's wine. Festivities include feasting, singing, and dancing.
- ✪ **INDEPENDENCE DAY**—National flags are out all over the country on October 28th, the day Czechoslovakia was formed in 1918.

Czechs love to wear colorful costumes during their festivals! You can see some of them at the Ride of the Kings on page 14.

7

THE CHRISTMAS SEASON

D o you ever wish Christmas would come more than once a year? Czech children are lucky. They have Christmas twice in December! Christmas celebrates both the birth of Jesus Christ and the start of winter. It's a time to exchange presents and enjoy the chilly weather by strolling through street markets that sell crafts, toys, and warm drinks. It's also a time to decorate the home with lights, candles, and wreaths.

Above: Children can have a ball in the snow!

Opposite: Musicians perform in Prague's Old Town Square on Christmas Day.

These children are ready for a toboggan ride.

8

Watch out for St. Nicholas

What do you know about jolly old St. Nick? In some countries, St. Nicholas is Santa Claus, who comes on the night of December 24th to bring presents to children. In the Czech Republic, however, St. Nicholas comes early. December 6th is St. Nicholas' Day, when people honor this Christian saint. All children look forward to it, except those who have been bad, because St. Nicholas might come to punish them.

Unlike Santa Claus, St. Nicholas doesn't come down the chimney; he walks right through the front door! He always comes before the smallest children go to bed, so everyone gets to see him. He doesn't stay long—just long enough to shout "Ho Ho Ho," drop off a big bag of presents, and ask children if they've been naughty or nice.

Angels and devils

St. Nicholas has two helpers—an angel and a devil. If you've been good, the angel gives you sweets and gifts from a bag of presents. If you've been bad, watch out! The devil might scoop you up and carry you away.

Christianity was introduced to the Czech lands in A.D. 863, and Czechs have celebrated St. Nicholas' Day ever since.

Christmas lights and live fish

Christmas Eve arrives three weeks after St. Nicholas' Day. By then, all the homes are colorful, bright, and warm with the season's spirit. Wreaths dipped in gold paint adorn people's doors, Christmas trees are decorated with lovely ornaments, and candles are placed on the window sills.

Everyone looks forward to the traditional Christmas meal, but Christmas dinner in the Czech Republic is probably a little different from what a lot of people are used to. A few days before Christmas, huge barrels full of water are rolled out onto street corners. If you peer inside, you'll see live fish swimming around! The traditional Christmas food is **carp**, fish raised in large ponds in southern Bohemia and Moravia. People buy live carp from the street-corner barrels and take them straight home to keep in their bathtubs until Christmas Day!

People buy live carp at a Christmas market. The traditional Christmas dinner begins with carp soup, followed by carp fried with bread crumbs or cooked in black sauce.

Christmas Eve is also called Generous Day. It is a wonderful time to exchange presents.

Think about this

All saints honored by the Catholic church have their own days on the Czech calendar. For people named after saints, these days are **name days**. A name day is almost like a second birthday to Czechs. So, if your name is Nicholas, December 6th is extra special because it is both your name day and a holiday.

CELEBRATIONS OF NEW LIFE

Czechs love spring. After a dreary winter, they look forward to this beautiful season, which heralds the arrival of fresh crops and new life.

Easter

Easter is a religious holiday commemorating the **resurrection** of Jesus Christ. It also celebrates the birth of spring, when grass and flowers start to grow, and baby chicks hatch in farmyards. During the week before Easter, children have lots of fun making crafts, such as painted eggs and paper flowers, and hanging colorful ribbons around the home.

On Easter Sunday, some families go to church. Then the whole family— uncles, aunts, cousins, and grandparents— gathers for a big midday meal of chicken and potatoes or roast beef and dumplings. For dessert, they eat Easter cake. After the meal, the children prepare for an unusual battle they will have the next day.

As spring approaches, Czechs start hanging Easter eggs around their homes.

Children like to watch grown-ups make traditional Easter cakes. Sometimes, they chip in and help, too.

Get out your sticks and water!

Easter Monday in the Czech Republic has an interesting twist.
On this day, boys and girls battle each other, using braided willow
sticks and buckets of water as weapons. The afternoon before the
battle, boys gather long, thin branches from willow trees, and girls
prepare buckets of water, which they hide in a secret corner
outside their homes. The next morning, the boys sneak up on the
girls and pretend to "whip" them with their willow sticks! They
don't hit hard because they don't want to hurt the girls. The girls,
in turn, throw buckets of water on the boys.

Where did such an unusual tradition come from, and what
does it mean? It is probably a **pagan** tradition—a festival
celebrated by the early Czech people who were not Christians and
had their own religious beliefs. These early Czechs were farmers,
and they believed that "whipping" a young girl with the wood of a
young willow tree ensured her **fertility**, or ability to produce
children later in life. Because these people were farmers and
worked the land without tractors, the more people in the family
who could help in the fields, the better. So this tradition is really a
celebration of new life.

13

Ride of the Kings

Welcome to the Ride of the Kings! Do you sometimes wish you could be a king or a queen, even for just one day? Well, young boys living in some towns in Moravia can be, because their towns have a unique festival called Ride of the Kings. This festival celebrates the new crops of spring and the progression of young boys into manhood. Because spring symbolizes a new beginning, Czechs hope that, by celebrating this festival, new crops will flourish and young boys will grow up to be good, strong men. This ancient tradition is now celebrated only in a few towns.

Before the "kings" ride, they spend about two days recruiting older men to help them decorate the horses.

Think about this
What is the significance of Easter eggs? Eggs symbolize birth, and Easter in the Czech Republic celebrates the beginning, or birth, of spring. Painting and displaying Easter eggs is a way to show that spring is coming.

Kings for a day!

During the last week of May, young boys invite some men in their villages to help each of them decorate a horse with paper flowers and ribbons. Then, on the last Sunday, the boys become "kings" for a day. They ride the decorated horses around the village with the men who helped them. In some villages, each of the "kings" has to clench a rose in his mouth because he is not allowed to talk or smile. Sometimes the "kings" are dressed in women's clothes. Why? According to an ancient belief, the women's clothes are supposed to protect new crops. Starting at one boy's home, the procession winds through the village. This festival is important for the boys, because, after the ride, all the men in their villages will accept them as adults. To celebrate the boys' claims to adulthood, there will be feasting, music, and dancing.

Above: In rural Moravia, harvest yields are very important to the people because their livelihood depends on good crops.

Below: When there are no festive celebrations, such as the Ride of the Kings, the town of Strážnice, in southern Moravia, is very quiet.

Prague Spring International Music Festival

I magine sitting in the garden of a grand palace, with a fountain gurgling behind you, and the stone spires of a 1,000-year-old cathedral on a hill rising high above you. A group of violinists dressed in white wigs and breeches appears on stage, and the soothing sound of a Mozart or Smetana quartet fills the air. **Aristocrats** and royalty lived this way hundreds of years ago, and music lovers today can have a similar experience at the Prague Spring International Music Festival.

Most young Czechs can play at least one musical instrument. Since violin playing is one of the oldest skills in the Czech Republic, many Czech children spend a good part of their childhood trying to master it.

The importance of music

Czechs, young and old, love music. Playing an instrument, singing, and dancing are considered essential parts of education, so children are always encouraged to study and listen to music. Because music is such an important part of Czech culture, there are lots of music festivals throughout the year, including folk music, rock, and jazz festivals. The grandest festival of them all is the Prague Spring International Music Festival.

Above: Musicians perform in the Villa Bertramka in Prague. The villa used to be the residence of the Dušeks, a family of musicians. It is now the Mozart Museum.

Buskers, or street musicians, play at the Staromeske square in Prague. The square is a popular gathering place for both musicians and music lovers.

Glorious surroundings

Prague, the Czech capital, is one of the most scenic cities in Europe, and it is at its most beautiful in May. The music festival there attracts thousands of music lovers from all over the world to enjoy the fine weather and scenery and to listen to famous musicians perform. Many of the concerts take place in the city's beautiful cathedral or in one of its **baroque** palaces or churches.

   The festival goes on for three weeks. During that time, an important music competition is held, focusing on a different instrument each year. The winner usually becomes a world-famous musician.

Above: This statue of Smetana, one of the Czech Republic's best-loved composers, can be found outside a theater near Charles Bridge in Prague.

Below: This band of musicians is entertaining passersby on the Charles Bridge, which overlooks the famous Vltava River.

A musical poem

The Prague Spring International Music Festival opens on the night of May 12th, the anniversary of famous Czech composer Bedřich Smetana's death. The festival starts with the dramatic performance of Smetana's *Má Vlast*, or *My Homeland*, a work known and loved by all Czechs almost as much as their national anthem. *Má Vlast* is a long musical poem that describes the flow of the Vltava River. In the beginning, flutes sound like water swirling through the rocky riverbeds of the mountains. Then, violins play the folk songs of the Bohemian farmlands, followed by sudden drumrolls that announce an approaching thunderstorm. Finally, trumpets proclaim the river's entry into the city of Prague.

The president of the Czech Republic usually attends the BBC Philharmonic Orchestra's performance of *Má Vlast* in Dvořák Hall on the opening night of the festival.

Think about this
Do you dance, sing, or play an instrument? Most Czech children do, because the Czechs believe that music runs through their veins. It is one of the most important aspects of their national culture. They even have a saying, "If you're Czech, then you're a musician."

19

CHRUDIM PUPPET FESTIVAL

M ost of the year, Chrudim is a sleepy town in eastern Bohemia. In early July, however, the streets of Chrudim are flooded with visitors who come to celebrate the craftsmanship of puppets.

Puppet-makers and **puppeteers**, or people who put on puppet shows, gather in Chrudim to demonstrate the tricks of their trade and to share in the **pageantry** of this unique craft. The highlight of this festival is a series of puppet shows that are short performances of popular stories. All of the actors are puppets.

Above: Puppet plays have been popular since the 16th century. These puppets are performing Mozart's opera *Don Giovanni*.

Below: Before the 20th century, puppet shows were considered children's entertainment. Now, even adults love to watch them.

Marionettes

Marionettes are string puppets. They are made from many pieces of wood held together with thin string or fishing line. Pull the strings from above, and the marionettes spring to life! Marionettes are dressed up in different clothes to represent soldiers, bakers, teachers, or nurses. They can look very real when controlled by a master puppeteer. Puppet shows tell funny stories, popular fairy tales, and folk tales in an amusing way.

The Chrudim Puppet Festival attracts puppeteers from all over the world.

Above: These marionettes are works of art. Look at the detailed craftsmanship.

Right: A street performer with leg puppets controls their movements using strings he holds in his hands.

You call that a puppet?

You might be surprised at how many different kinds of puppets there are and how creative some people can be with them. Puppets can be made from socks that you wear on your hand, from pieces of wood and string, or even from your own body! Czechs love to watch street artists perform plays using their own legs as puppets. These artists paint a female figure on one leg and a male figure on the other. Then, using a piece of cloth as the stage curtain, they dance to classical or pop music. Some do it so well that their leg puppets look like two separate dancers moving to a waltz or disco.

A living tradition

Czechs have a long tradition of making beautiful puppets. Little children love to play with them, adults like to brighten up their homes with them. With a little imagination, there are many interesting stories that can be told with these colorful figures in hand.

Like the many baroque palaces and churches in the Czech Republic, puppet shows have a long history. Czechs adore puppet theater because they see it as the perfect expression of folklife. Closely tied to their folk traditions, Czechs would naturally have a special festival for puppets. If, however, you miss the puppet festival in Chrudim, you can always visit the puppet museum there.

These children at a nursery school in Prague are being treated to a puppet show.

Think about this
Which famous puppets do you know? How about Pinocchio? He's a marionette. Kermit the Frog? He's a hand puppet, made from an old green coat. Think of your favorite story, then make puppets of the characters and put on your own puppet show.

BURNING OF THE WITCHES

Czechs believe witches are evil spirits, so they try to make witch effigies look hideous.

Do you like witches? Or are you afraid of them? Either way, you should visit the Czech Republic on the night of April 30th to see the Burning of the Witches.

Evil spirits

Winter in the Czech Republic is very long. People say that the evil spirit of witches keeps everything cold and dark. To welcome spring, Czechs get together to burn the witch that kept winter around so long. They don't burn a real witch, of course; they burn an **effigy**, or likeness, of a witch, made of straw, old clothes, and broomsticks.

Below: Czech children enjoy the outdoors despite the cold.

The bonfire

On the evening of April 30th, Czechs gather to build a bonfire and prepare the witch effigy. First, they tie two large sticks together to form a cross. Then they stuff old shirts, pants, and socks with straw and place a pointed hat on the top of the stack. The witch is tied to a broomstick and set aside until darkness falls.

When the fire is roaring, people roast sausages on sticks, strum guitars, and sing their favorite songs. Everyone looks forward to nightfall, when they will face the spirits of the witches. As soon as it's dark, the witch effigy is brought out and held up for all to see. Then, with a heave of the arm, it is thrown on top of the fire. As the witch burns, so does the last of winter's chill.

Czechs used to believe that the power of witches would weaken as the weather got warmer. So they thought that if they made something that looked like a witch and burned it, they could finally get rid of the cold winter.

Think about this

Can you think of a festival like the Burning of the Witches in your own country? How about Halloween? Halloween is a night when people try to drive away evil spirits. Some even dress up to imitate these spirits. Czechs don't have Halloween, but the Burning of the Witches is very similar.

THINGS FOR YOU TO DO

Czechs make crafts from common items they have around the house and garden. They love to make things, especially in the spring and summer when they spend time at their cottages in the countryside. It's amazing how they can turn simple objects into creative and funny toys. Here are two ideas for animal figures you can make from fruits and vegetables.

Lemon pig

To make a lemon pig, you will need a lemon, four toothpicks, paper, colored pencils, scissors, and glue. Imagine that the two ends of a lemon are the nose and tail of a pig. Stick four toothpicks into the lemon to make the pig's legs. Draw eyes on pieces of paper, cut them out, and glue them onto the lemon. Make ears by cutting triangular pieces of paper and coloring them pink. Then attach each ear to the lemon by folding the base and gluing it in place.

Cucumber crocodile

To make a cucumber crocodile, you will need a cucumber, paper, colored pencils, scissors, and glue. Cut a strip of paper about 8 inches x 1 inch (20 centimeters x 2.5 centimeters) and draw teeth along the strip. Glue the strip over one end of the cucumber, so that it looks like a mouth. Then, draw and cut out small circles to make eyes. Glue the eyes above the ends of the mouth. Now you have the head of a crocodile. There are lots of animals you can make from other fruits and vegetables. See which ones you can create!

Things to look for in your library

Arts and Culture and the Czech Republic. (http://sunsite.mff.cuni.cz/czechrep/culture/Index.html, 1996).

Czech Republic. Cultures of the World (series). Efstathia Sioras (Marshall Cavendish Corporation, 1999).

Czech Republic—Country Insights, City and Village Life. Rob Humphreys (Raintree/Steck-Vaughn, 1998).

Czech Republic in Pictures. Visual Geography (series). (Lerner Publications, 1995).

Czechland: A Czech Culture-Heritage Website. (http://www.czechland.org/index.html, 1998).

Favorite Fairy Tales Told in Czechoslovakia. Virginia Haviland (Beech Tree Books, 1995).

The Palaces of Prague. Zdeněk Hojda and Jiří Pešek (Vendome Press, 1995).

Romantic Prague. (Madacy Entertainment, 1998).

MAKE A CHRISTMAS CHAIN

Making Christmas tree ornaments is a popular winter pastime for Czechs. It's easy to do, and the ornaments make the house look great. Here's an ornament project for you to try.

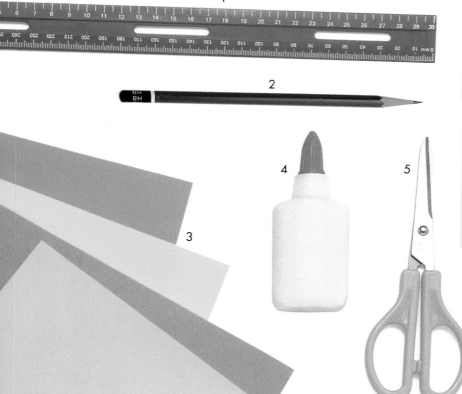

1

2

4

5

3

You will need:
1. Ruler
2. Pencil
3. Colored paper (many colors)
4. Paste or glue
5. Scissors

1 Draw lines on colored paper to make strips. Each strip should measure 5" x ½" (12.5 cm x 1.3 cm). You will need at least fifty strips, but the more you have, the longer your chain will be.

2 Cut out the paper strips.

3 Form one strip into a ring by pasting one end of it to the other. Slip another strip of paper (use a different color) through the first ring and paste the ends of it together. Repeat these steps with each strip, always attaching a new ring to the last one formed. You can drape your Christmas chain around the Christmas tree or across the ceiling.

MAKE BRAMBORÁK

A favorite snack in the Czech Republic is *bramborák* (BRAHM-bo-rahk), or potato pancake. Czechs enjoy eating them at festival time and at family gatherings.

You will need:

1. Frying pan
2. 2 ounces (57 g) flour
3. ½ teaspoon salt
4. ½ teaspoon pepper
5. 1 egg
6. 1 clove garlic, crushed
7. ½ teaspoon majoram
8. Oven mitt
9. Mixing bowl
10. 2½ tablespoons milk
11. 2 tablespoons cooking oil
12. 1 pound (464 g) grated potatoes
13. Wooden spoon
14. Pancake turner
15. Measuring spoons

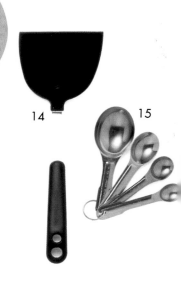

1 Mix together the flour, milk, egg, garlic, salt, pepper, and marjoram.

2 Add the potatoes to this mixture and blend thoroughly.

3 Form patties with the mixture. Then, ask an adult to help you fry them with cooking oil in the frying pan. When the patties are brown, serve and eat!

GLOSSARY

aristocrats, 16	Members of noble families.
baroque, 18	The elaborate architectural style of palaces and churches built in the 16th century.
carp, 11	A kind of large freshwater fish.
commemorate, 6	To remember a person or an event with a ceremony or festival.
effigy, 24	A crude representation of a person made from common items.
fertility, 13	The ability to have children.
Middle Ages, 4	The period of history in Europe from the 5th century to the 15th century.
name days, 11	Special calendar days, each of which honors a Christian saint of a particular name.
pagan, 13	A person who has few, if any, religious beliefs or believes in many gods.
pageantry, 20	Colorful, spectacular ceremonies or shows.
puppeteer, 20	A person who performs with puppets.
resurrection, 12	Act of rising from the dead.

INDEX